LOOKING INTO THE
RAIN FOREST

BY EMMA HUDDLESTON

The Child's World®

childsworld.com

Published by The Child's World®
1980 Lookout Drive • Mankato, MN 56003-1705
800-599-READ • www.childsworld.com

Photographs ©: iStockphoto, cover (background), cover (macaw), 1 (background), 1 (macaw), 2 (background), 8, 11, 12, 17, 24; ABDesign/iStockphoto, cover (frog), 1 (frog), 2 (frog), 21; Save Jungle/Shutterstock Images, 5; Ramdan Nain/iStockphoto, 6; MD Zahid Hasan/Shutterstock Images, 9; Reise Graf/iStockphoto, 13; Travel Strategy/iStockphoto, 14; Pedro Helder Pinheiro/Shutterstock Images, 16; Damian Pankowiec/Shutterstock Images, 19

ISBN 9781503835214
LCCN 2019943116

Printed in the United States of America

ABOUT THE AUTHOR

Emma Huddleston is a children's book author. She lives in Minnesota with her husband. She enjoys learning about the world in which we live while she writes.

TABLE OF CONTENTS

CHAPTER ONE

Rain Forests Have Layers

The green treetops of the Amazon rain forest cover thousands of miles. Hawks fly above the trees. Monkeys swing from vines. Colorful flowers bloom.

Tropical rain forests are warm and wet. They get 80 to 400 inches (200 to 1,000 cm) of rain each year. When it is not raining, **humidity** keeps the area wet. Tropical rain forests are found in places such as South and Central America, Africa, and Indonesia. They are located near the **equator**. The equator gets lots of sunlight. Temperatures range from 70 to 85 degrees Fahrenheit (20 to 30°C).

Tropical rain forests have four layers. The top layer is the emergent layer. Beneath it lie the canopy and understory layers. The forest floor is the bottom layer. The layers of a rain forest are home to **diverse** plant and animal life.

Layers of a Rain Forest

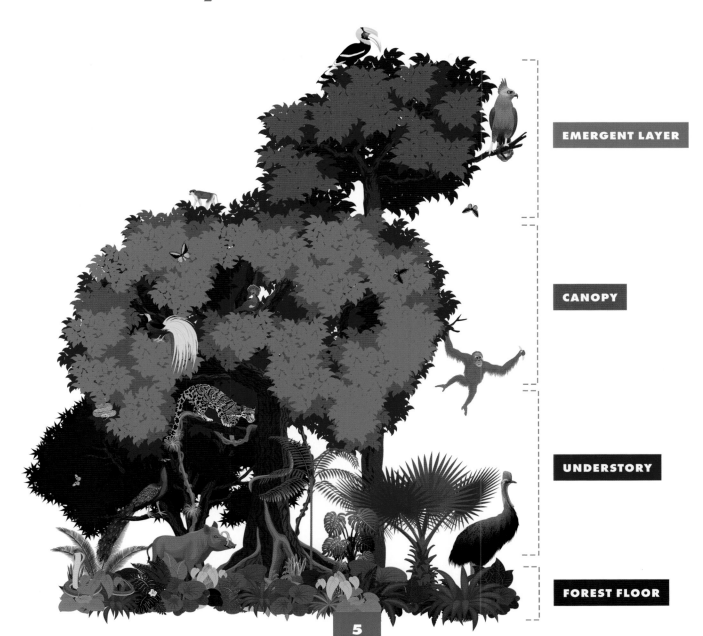

EMERGENT LAYER

CANOPY

UNDERSTORY

FOREST FLOOR

Emergent trees tower over the rain forest.

CHAPTER TWO

The Emergent Layer

The emergent layer is the highest layer in a tropical rain forest. It is where the tallest trees reach up into the sky. Some grow up to 200 feet (60 m) tall.

Trees in this layer benefit from the sun, rain, and wind. Their branches and leaves spread out at the top. This lets them take in more rain and sunlight. The rain and sunlight help the trees grow. The wind helps trees spread their seeds. Many trees in this layer have small, light seeds. They are easily blown by the wind.

The kapok tree grows in rain forests of Central and South America and Africa. It has no lower branches. All its branches grow from the top of the trunk. They spread out in an umbrella shape. The tree's seeds are connected to pale, thin fibers. These tangles of fibers carry the seeds.

Many butterflies live in rain forests. A blue morpho butterfly's wings can span 5 to 8 inches (13 to 20 cm).

In the emergent layer, the hot sun and strong winds can dry out trees' bark and leaves. One way trees survive is with tough, waxy leaves. They store water. They protect the tree from drying out.

Most animals move through the emergent layer by flying, gliding, or swinging. Birds, bats, and insects fly through rain forests around the world. Pygmy gliders are small marsupials that live in New Guinea. They glide through the air using flaps of skin between their front and back legs. Gibbon apes are another animal found in the emergent layer. They rarely spend time on the ground. They swing through trees in the rain forests of Southeast Asia.

Gliders such as this sugar glider soar from tree to tree. They use their tails to steer.

CHAPTER THREE

The Canopy

Under the emergent layer is the canopy. In the canopy, many tree branches and leaves twist together. It is **dense**. This means the trees are very close together. The canopy layer is about 20 feet (6 m) thick. It includes trees of multiple heights.

The air in this layer is still. The many trees block the wind from flowing through. The canopy is damp. Water drips down from leaf to leaf. Trees in the canopy have glossy leaves with pointed tips. This lets water drip easily off them. It keeps water moving down the layers. It also keeps the leaves dry. If they are dry, mold will not grow on them. Mold can make trees sick and even kill them.

Many types of orchids grow up in the canopy. Their roots get water from the air.

The canopy is active. Most animals in tropical rain forests live in this layer. Monkeys move by swinging or leaping. Birds fly from branch to branch. Many animals in the canopy make loud noises. Their noises travel through the dense trees. The shouting howler monkey and shrieking scarlet macaw live in the Amazon canopy. They must be loud for other monkeys and macaws to hear them. Other animals stay quiet. Sloths rarely make noise. They live alone.

Howler monkeys use their call to say what area of the canopy is theirs.

A toucan's long bill allows it to reach for fruit on branches.

In the canopy, wind cannot spread seeds. So, many seeds grow in fruits. Fruit is food for many animals. The animals eat it and travel to different locations. When the animals poop, they spread the trees' seeds.

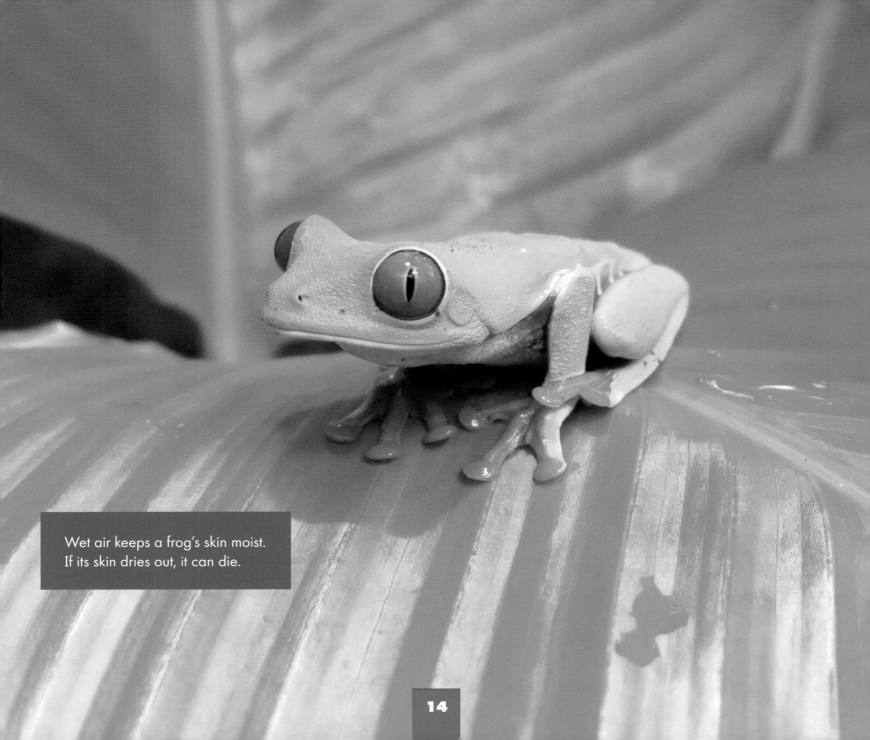

Wet air keeps a frog's skin moist. If its skin dries out, it can die.

CHAPTER FOUR

The Understory

The understory is several feet below the canopy. It includes young trees and short plants. The canopy forms a roof over the understory. This makes the understory dark and cool. The canopy blocks almost all wind, sunlight, and rainfall. The air in this layer is still and humid. It feels sticky.

Moss grows well in this layer. It needs cool, damp surroundings. The other layers have too much sun for moss to grow. However, many other plants need sunlight to survive. That is why most plants in the understory have large leaves. Palms are common in this layer. Their large leaves catch the small amount of sunlight that gets through the dense canopy.

Plants also survive in the understory by attracting insects. Insects spread pollen from flower to flower. This helps plants create new seeds. Some plants use large flowers to attract insects. Other flowers have a strong smell. The smell helps insects find them in the dark.

The spots on a Jaguar's coat help it blend in.

The largest flower in the world is *Rafflesia*. It grows in Southeast Asia. It is more than 3 feet (1 m) across. The flower smells like rotting meat. This smell attracts flies. The flies bring pollen to the flower.

Animals such as frogs and snakes live in the understory. Many use **camouflage** to blend into their surroundings. The dim light benefits them. These animals can hide from predators. And camouflaged predators can sneak up on the animals they are hunting.

Jungles vs. Rain Forests

Jungles are much like rain forests. The main difference between the two is where they are densest. Rain forests have dense canopies. Their understories are dim and open. Jungles are dense in lower layers. The trees grow farther apart. This lets more light into the bottom layers. Because of the sunlight, more plants grow low to the ground.

CHAPTER FIVE

The Forest Floor

The forest floor is the bottom layer of a tropical rain forest. The forest floor is the darkest layer. It gets little to no sunlight. This makes it hard for plants to grow. The soil on the forest floor does not have many **nutrients**. The nutrients have been moved away by natural forces such as water. But plants need nutrients to grow. For this reason, **decomposers** are a key part of the forest floor.

Decomposers such as **fungi** and worms break down plant and animal waste into nutrients. This puts nutrients back on top of the soil. To get nutrients, plants in rain forests spread their roots wide instead of deep. The shallow roots can reach the nutrients in the top layers of the soil.

Fungi grow best in shaded, moist areas.

Animals on the forest floor hunt and dig for food. Snakes, wild pigs, and anteaters live in this layer. Creatures such as snails and termites also live there. Termites break down wood and dead leaves. Without termites, piles of dead wood and leaves would build up. Nutrients would not be put back into the soil as quickly. Plant life in the rain forest could struggle to survive.

Each layer of the rain forest supports life. The top layers of a rain forest affect the amount of sunlight, water, and airflow in the lower layers. Plants and animals need the rain forest for food, water, and shelter. They depend on each layer. Rain forests help millions of living creatures survive.

FAST FACTS

- Tropical rain forests have warm and wet climates.

- Tropical rain forests have four layers: the emergent layer, canopy, understory, and forest floor.

- The emergent layer is the highest. Trees in this layer get the most sunlight, rain, and wind.

- The canopy is very dense. The trees shelter the layers below.

- The understory is dim because of the canopy. Plants there have large leaves that take in as much sunlight as possible.

- The forest floor gets little to no sunlight.

- Decomposers break down matter and return nutrients to the top layer of soil.

GLOSSARY

camouflage (KAM-uh-flahzh) Camouflage is colors or patterns that blend in with the surroundings. Frogs use camouflage to hide.

decomposers (dee-kuhm-POH-zurz) Decomposers are living things that break down dead things. Termites are decomposers.

dense (DENSS) Dense means heavy or packed together. The canopy is dense with tree branches.

diverse (dy-VURSS) Diverse means having many different types. Rain forests have diverse plants.

equator (i-KWAY-tur) The equator is an imaginary line around the middle of Earth. It is warm near the equator.

fungi (FUHN-gy) Fungi are like plants but have no leaves, flowers, or roots. Fungi grow on the forest floor.

humidity (hyoo-MID-uh-tee) Humidity is water in the air. Rain forests have a high humidity.

nutrients (NOO-tree-unts) Nutrients are what living things need to stay healthy. Plants use nutrients in the soil.

TO LEARN MORE

IN THE LIBRARY

Fullman, Joe. *3-D Explorer: Rain Forest*. San Diego, CA: Silver Dolphin Books, 2018.

Gibbs, Maddie. *What Are Tropical Rainforests?* New York, NY: Britannica Educational Publishing, 2019.

Ringstad, Arnold. *Rain Forest Habitats*. Mankato, MN: The Child's World, 2014.

ON THE WEB

Visit our website for links about rain forests:

childsworld.com/links

Note to Parents, Teachers, and Librarians: We routinely verify our Web links to make sure they are safe and active sites. So encourage your readers to check them out!

INDEX